KEEP THE MEMORIES, NOT THE STUFF

JEANNINE BRYANT

Special thanks to:
Cover designer & graphic artist Ashley Erks
Editor Linda Stephen

Get more rightsizing tips, information, and inspiration at www.EasyRightsizing.com

TABLE OF CONTENTS

INTRODUCTION

"We all get organized eventually, we just might not be around for it."
-Sue DeRoos, professional organizer

The brutal reality is that people die, and their stuff must go somewhere. It's often up to those they leave behind to decide where that somewhere is. Professional organizer Sue DeRoos has astutely observed that "we all get organized eventually, we just might not be around for it."

This quote has been an invaluable teaching tool in my work as a senior move manager over the last decade. I have worked with hundreds of clients who were downsizing to a smaller home, townhouse, or apartment. I've also worked with hundreds of families who were emptying out the home of a loved one who had died. The reason I use this quote from Sue DeRoos is that it reminds us that the issue of *"What to do with all this stuff?"* is a question that every one of us must answer at one point in our lives. Either we deal with our own possessions or someone else will have to deal with them after we are gone. Chances are high that you'll find yourself in the position of having to extend this help to loved ones, as they empty out their home or apartment someday.

The advice in this book is important to me not only because I have made a career out of helping people rightsize their belongings, but because I've experienced the burden of too much stuff in my own family. I have seen how heavily excess stuff weighs on the shoulders of my loved ones throughout my life.

As a child, I watched my parents empty out my grandparents' homes after their deaths in 1992 and 1994. My parents were in their 40s at the time, coming off a grueling several years of caring for aging parents, raising two small children, and working hard to grow their farming operation in the prime of their careers. I grew up in rural North Dakota, where people have not only houses filled with stuff, but entire farmsteads with outbuildings (barns, sheds, garages, and even old chicken coops) filled with stuff. After burying their parents, and in the midst of grieving them, my mom and dad spent several months (time they didn't have) emptying out two farmsteads' worth of stuff. Most of it went in the trash. My grandparents died, their houses were emptied, and hired farm employees moved in.

In 2005, my mother died, and it became clear that my father didn't intend to stay in their big empty house, full of stuff and memories, for long. The farm was my father's domain, and the house was my mother's. So, when it came time for my father to move off the farm and into town, he didn't intend to keep much. I found myself, at the age of 24, sorting through my mother's possessions to identify what I wanted to keep and figure out what should be done with the rest. I sifted through her papers, the books she never read, the projects only half-finished, the clothing she would never wear again.

We donated much of it. But when the house was sold and my dad moved into town, there was still a whole lot that went into storage. Fifteen years later, some of my parents' stuff still sits in storage. "Some things are just meant to be kept until after I die," my father says in a gruff, joking manner. These are the things he's not yet ready to part with.

In a professional capacity, for the last decade, I have owned a senior move management company in Lincoln, Nebraska called Changing Spaces SRS. Our Changing Spaces team of 20 helps hundreds of seniors and their families through times of transition each and every year. As clients move to a new, smaller space in a condo or retirement community, we help them with sorting, packing, managing move day, unpacking, and organizing their new home. We also organize and run estate sales and online auctions to help clients and their families to empty out their old home quickly. We also frequently work with families who are using our services after the death of a loved one.

We see first-hand the impact stuff has on our aging clients and on the grieving families we help. I encourage all of us to make this process easier by "rightsizing" our belongings as we go through our lives – not waiting until moving day to clear out 40 years' worth of business papers or 50 years' worth of holiday décor.

I am so passionate about the process of rightsizing, in fact, that I wrote a book to help any homeowner in the midst of such a process. *Ready to Rightsize?* is available on my website www.EasyRightsizing.com, along with many other free resources including videos, podcasts, worksheets, and blog articles. Watch my videos with hints on sorting through clutter in a kitchen or closet, reducing paperwork piles in an office, and more.

I am not a trained grief counselor, but I do lead a team of caring people who have walked alongside hundreds of families as they liquidate the possessions of a loved one who has died. I've seen it all. I've seen families handle this difficult process with ease and grace, and I've seen families struggle and fight throughout. I've seen families clutch, with desperation, to their loved ones' belongings because they were unable to let go. They hang on to the stuff as though it were a life preserver. In my role as an objective third party, it is easy to see that the stuff is actually an anchor weighing families down and preventing them from living in the present.

I don't want you to be weighed down by your stuff, or by your loved ones' stuff. I want for you, dear reader, a lightness, a healthy connection to keepsake items and family memorabilia, but not such a tight grip that the objects prevent you from letting go and moving on. When it comes to your keepsakes, I want you to keep the best (and ONLY the best) and let go of the rest.

I want you to keep the memories, not the stuff.

PART I: THE WEIGHT OF INHERITED STUFF

CHAPTER 1. MY LOVED ONE DIED. NOW WHAT?

It will be one of the worst times of your life, and it will require so much from you. When a loved one dies, there are so many decisions to make all at once: forms to fill out, a funeral to plan, documents to file, people to notify, logins and passwords to discover, accounts to close. All of these tasks must be done while grieving the passing of someone you loved. This is not a book about grief, but it is a book about stuff, and so often the two are very much intertwined.

Immediately after a death, our loved ones' things become precious. When my mother died in 2005, every scrap of paper we could find with her handwriting, every card she gave us, even the last grocery list she penned became precious. I gathered every photograph of her I could find. Her clothing in the closets and drawers that still smelled like her and her cell phone that still played her voicemail greeting when we called it, these things felt like life preservers in the midst of the most terrible storm any of us had experienced. We were gutted by the loss, unsure of how any of us would continue our lives without her.

Once the funeral has passed and you are able to catch your breath, the issue of what to do with the deceased's possessions is bound to come up. Whether the deceased lived in a house, an apartment, a retirement community or a nursing home, your loved one's residence will need to be emptied out in one way or another. You won't be able to sell the home, or give up the lease, until you do. For many of the people I've worked with, this financial incentive lights a fire under them, and they want to empty out what's left in a hurry.

This doesn't happen easily.

Oftentimes, cleaning out is a task that must be done in between episodes of crying, sobbing, questioning, regretting, remembering, and a whole host of other emotions that emerge in those first weeks and months after losing a loved one. Emptying a home is a task that would be difficult anyway, but when done in the midst of a hurricane of emotions, it becomes insurmountable at times.

For this reason, some people put off the process of emptying out a loved one's home. They either pack everything in the home and move it to their own basement, garage, or storage unit where it will sit and take up precious space for months or years. Or, if there are no pressing financial reasons to empty out and sell the home (or give up the lease), it seems easier to just let things lay for a while. I don't fault families who choose this route – in fact, it might be best, psychologically and emotionally, to do this. It gives you time to breathe and grieve before turning your attention to the practical aspects of emptying out a home.

However, I've also seen situations where the family waits too long, thinking that they aren't ready to deal with the stuff. Pretty soon it has been years since their loved one has passed and the home still sits, full and undisturbed. I want to tell you that you'll never be completely ready to empty out the home of someone you loved, but that doesn't mean you can put it off forever.

What I see so often with grown children who wait years to take on this step is a reluctance to let go. The house and its contents have become a shrine to the person or people they loved most in the world. In many cases, these homes are the very place where the adult children spent their childhoods, which adds another layer of complexity to the situation.

What I've said to people in these situations is this: *What you really want is not all this stuff. What you want is for your parents to be alive again and thriving in this place. You want this house to be a home again – the home you remember.* I understand. This is what I want, too. It's what all of us who have lost parents want – but we can't have it. It's the difficult part of growing up. You lose your parents, and in a way, you lose both your childhood and part of your past with them.

Leaving our loved one's home and belongings untouched creates a kind of museum of the past, which can be comforting for a while – in the first weeks and months after you've lost somebody. But there's a turning point in the grieving process, isn't there? There comes a point when it no longer makes you feel good to go over and visit this museum dedicated to the memory of someone you've lost. It just makes it sadder. It's easy to be scared that if you empty out the place, you'll forget – forget what it felt like to be in this home, to smell the familiar smells, to see things on the walls and on the shelves just where our loved one put them.

This is meant to be a comforting sentiment but also a call to action: There are no set timelines or rules for how this process should work. YOU get to decide, YOU are in charge. However, while you are the one who gets to decide how to proceed, you are also the one who will need to act, sooner or later. The authority to decide comes with the responsibility to act.

Will this happen all at once? Probably not, and it shouldn't. Emptying out a loved one's home will likely happen in phases, uncovering items in layers. You'll feel like an archeologist at times, and I'm willing to bet you will uncover more than a few surprising things. That's quite common, and I think that this process of emptying out a home can really serve as a kind of therapy after losing your loved one. It can be an instrument to help you along the mourning process if you let it.

I've broken down the overwhelming process of emptying out a home into five stages to make it easier for my clients. Believe it or not, all of the items in every home will fall into one of these five categories: keep, give away, sell, donate or trash. You can learn more about this step-by-step process through my resources at www.EasyRightsizing.com. An illustration of this process is provided here, to help readers remember that identifying the items in each category should always be done in order.

The five stages
of emptying a home.

When emptying out a home, you always begin at the top, deciding which items you are going to KEEP and which items you will GIVE AWAY to family or friends. After that, you move on to SELL what you can, DONATE what is useful to charity, and DISPOSE of the trash/recycling left in the home. Again, for a further discussion of this process, watch the videos explaining each step at www.EasyRightsizing.com.

What we will focus on in this book are the items that fall into the "keep" and "give" categories. Determining what you will keep and give to family or friends must always be the first step. Too often I have seen people's ideas bounce around from deciding what to donate to charity, to estimating how much money they think they can get from their loved one's antique collection, to thinking about throwing out the trash and the empty cardboard boxes from the basement. When you bounce around like this, it's very difficult to make any real progress.

If you have recently lost a loved one, I want to take you gently by the shoulders, look you in the eye, and tell you to first <u>focus simply on what you want to keep and what you will give to family and friends.</u> Until that is determined, everything else is wasted energy. And once that is determined, it makes all the other steps so much easier.

Determining what you truly WANT to keep should be easy. Ask yourself, if no one else's opinion mattered, what would I want to take out of this house and put into mine? If I weren't worrying about others' expectations of me, of pleasing my family members or letting my grief cloud my judgement, what would I keep? If the house were on fire and I had 10 minutes to collect everything that truly mattered the most, what would I take? It's these kinds of exercises that can be really helpful in articulating what matters most to you. Listen to your answers without the expectations and opinions of others weighing on you.

After determining which items you will keep, you can begin thinking about what items should be given to family/friends. Ask them what items they want (i.e. Grandmother's needlepoint picture) and which items they could use (i.e. Grandmother's crockpot, since theirs broke last week). Families have tackled this process of dividing in a variety of ways, and so much depends on the particular dynamics of your family. Do you anticipate multiple family members vying for the same items? Or do you doubt that members of your family will want much of anything? Some families have an easier time dividing items up than others, and you likely know which camp your family will fall into.

If you anticipate some contention on who gets what, then approach the situation with a plan. The responsibility of dividing assets often falls on whoever was named executor of the deceased's will. This is no easy task, and the responsibility should not be taken lightly. Approaching the situation with an unbiased plan will help the process go more smoothly. Some families make it into a game – everyone draws a card and the one with the highest card decides first an item that they would like to have, then the one with the second highest card chooses, and so on. Others draw straws. Perhaps you'll decide to go in birth order – oldest first, youngest last. Develop a system that will work for your particular situation.

It's often best to include only immediate family members in this process (no in-laws allowed), then children, grandchildren and so forth. Some families are very concerned with keeping everything "equal" and others are not as concerned about that. Some families want a lot of items from their loved ones' homes, while others hardly want any items at all.

You'll need to decide what works best for your family's situation. Above all, remember to place the highest importance on PEOPLE, not STUFF. Your loved one will not be honored if there ends up being struggle and strife in the family over their possessions. You can try to be as fair as you can, but even if things get divided up in a way that you perceive as *unfair,* I encourage you to put the relationship above all else. Sometimes, the most noble thing you can do is simply to let it go. Remember, it's just stuff.

Dividing up the "keep" items is the first step of clearing out an estate, and if there is a reasonable amount of stuff that you genuinely want, this step can be the easiest. But what about all the items that you're not so sure about? These are the items that fall into the grey area. Perhaps you feel like you should keep them, but you're not sure you have the space to keep them, or even the desire. You may find yourself wanting to keep items out of obligation or fear of losing the memory. Herein lies the challenge that we will discuss in the coming chapters.

Chapter 2. Mourning, Grief, and Our Attachment to Stuff

Why is it so difficult to sort through the items that belonged to a loved one after they are gone? After someone we love dies, it can be one of the greatest sources of comfort to be with their things. To be in their home, drive their car, and sit amongst their possessions helps us feel, if only for a moment, close to them in a way that we know, deep down, will never be possible again. It hurts so much.

Sorting through and making decisions about a person's stuff forces you to come face to face with your relationship with them. After a loved one is gone, we can no longer change anything about our past relationship. It is what it is. Gone are the chances to give appreciation, to make amends, to apologize, or to ask questions. That is difficult – no matter what the state of the relationship was. Good or bad, the finality of the situation strikes us hard and keeps hitting us as we sort through all our loved ones' earthly possessions and determine what we are going to do.

Settling a loved one's estate, cleaning out the residence, and getting rid of the stuff – all of this closes a chapter on your relationship to that person and their life. It is letting go of the hope that your relationship, whatever it may have been, will ever be any different. It is over. It is what it was.

Many times, our answer to this difficult process is simply procrastination and indecision. We box up the items and put them away – in the basement, attic, or our garage. We delay the decisions because they seem too overwhelming to deal with at the time and filled with too much emotion.

Other times, we keep items that belonged to our loved ones out of guilt. We know that these items meant a lot to the person we have lost, and it feels disrespectful to get rid of them. We try to honor our loved one by honoring their possessions. But ARE we actually honoring our loved one by doing this? To honor is to regard with great respect. We can honor our loved one's memory by using or displaying the stuff they left behind, but if all we are doing is keeping their things in boxes, stored and hidden away, that's not honoring. That's storing.

Saying goodbye to the home itself can be a difficult process, particularly if your loved one lived there for many years. If it is your parents' home you are emptying out, this may be the very house you grew up in, the house that all the grandchildren knew as "grandma and grandpa's house." It may have been the location of many family gatherings, holidays, and celebrations. Letting go of a house like this is the end of an era. This will change where your family gathers and the way it celebrates. Oftentimes adult siblings drift apart after both parents have passed away. Cousins grow up, get married, or move away. Holidays won't be the same and traditions will evolve and change.

Besides procrastination, the fear of forgetting is also what motivates us to keep things. We worry that we might forget Dad's war stories if we let go of the military uniform. We worry we might not remember Grandma's special recipes if we don't keep the china dishes that the food was served on for decades. And this doesn't just pertain to the possessions of a deceased person, either. As parents with grown children, we worry that we might forget what it felt like to hold our babies in our arms if we let go of their onesies and stuffed animals long after they have outgrown them. We cling to the past by holding on to the stuff. The reality, however, is that stuff doesn't hold memories; people do.

People
hold memories,
stuff does not.

What we really want in each of these scenarios is for everything to be the way it used to be. We want time to stay frozen in one place. We want our kids to be little again, for our loved one to still be alive, for Mom and Dad or Grandma and Grandpa to be healthy and thriving once again in their home. But it doesn't work. That time is over. Keeping the home and a loved one's possessions like a museum won't return you to another time. At first keeping these objects may be comforting, but eventually, those things will become stale and sad. They will make you feel the loss of that person or that period in time even more.

So, what are we to do? We have to go through the stuff. We have to sort, and we have to let go. This has to be done for practical reasons or for legal matters. If done right, it can also serve an emotional purpose and help you work through your grief.

The secret is a positive mindset, an intention to search for happy memories, and a sense of appreciation amongst your loved one's items. When you actively look for happy memories amongst their stuff, the process can be as soothing to the soul as a balm. When sorting through kitchens, living rooms, basements, and closets, look for the joy. Look for the memories. Look for insights into your loved one's personality or parts of their lives that you may not have known before.

Not all memories will be happy ones. This is true for every person and every relationship. But now is the time to keep the things that make you smile rather than draw a tear. You won't be able to change your relationship with the person who is gone, but you can edit your memories and choose to save the happy ones – and to let go of the hurtful ones.

Another secret to success is to approach the entire project with an eye on the future. Nothing traps us in the past more than sorting through a deceased loved one's possessions. The memories pull us back in time and leave us enveloped in nothing but memories. This can be comforting for a while, but without a hope, vision, or plan for what the future holds, the past can be a pretty depressing place to reside. So, while you are remembering your loved one by sorting through their stuff, remember to pull yourself out of the project once in a while to re-enter the present world. Do something fun: take a walk, watch a movie, visit the zoo, or talk to friends and family that are still alive and with you.

As hard as it may be, find something in the future that you can plan for or look forward to. This future treat can be a little thing or a big thing – an upcoming vacation to recover from the stress of this project, or simply a glass of wine with a friend at the end of a long day. You must ground yourself in the present and look forward to the future, lest you find yourself trapped in the past with only memories of someone who is gone.

Enfold the entire experience with a whole lot of grace for both yourself and your deceased loved one, and you'll make it through just fine.

CHAPTER 3. WHAT WILL PEOPLE THINK?

Losing a loved one and realizing that it is now your responsibility to deal with all their earthly possessions can feel like a monumental weight on your shoulders. Not only is it logistically a huge task that you must fit in and around your already full schedule, but it is also emotionally draining to sort through the items that belonged to someone you loved and have now lost.

When you think of the responsibility that goes along with passing on your loved one's legacy to future generations, the pressure can be downright immobilizing. Mix that in with the expectations of others around you, and you just might have a recipe for disaster. What will society, my siblings, the neighbors, and my community say about this process?

If you are an only child dealing with emptying out your parents' house, that is a unique burden onto itself. No one to bounce ideas off of, ask for reassurance from, or gauge their opinion. But when you do have siblings or other family members helping to empty the house, there can be other challenges. Their opinions may differ from yours on how much, or what, to keep. Their way of processing all of this may be different, and that could make things more difficult.

Having a sibling that is more (or less) sentimental than you are can complicate things. Disagreements can occur, which can bring up hard feelings about past relational issues. Suddenly you can find yourself in a screaming match, apparently arguing about what should be done with Dad's golf clubs, but really arguing about feeling misunderstood and underappreciated your whole life.

Your relationship to your loved one at the time of their death will most certainly factor into the way you approach cleaning out their home. Perhaps you were the local daughter who has spent the last several years caring for aging parents, while your out-of-state siblings were living their lives with little connection to what was going on back home. Or perhaps you are the out-of-state child of a deceased parent, and you find yourself highly motivated to tie up the loose ends of your parents' estate because of the weight you feel of it hanging over your head. Whatever the situation may be, remember to put PEOPLE over

STUFF, and remember that everyone approaches the grieving process from a different place.

Others involved may have expectations of how the inherited stuff should be dealt with (everything from a set of Christmas china to a collection of beer mugs, a classic car, or the house itself). Friends and family will likely have an opinion on how fast, or how slow, the process of emptying out the house should be. They may be aghast if you clean the house out too quickly, or impatient and judgmental if it takes longer than they think it should. They will likely share these opinions with you. Try to remember whose opinions should count and whose should not.

The person who has the legal responsibility for closing out the estate is the one who truly has the power to make the decisions. That person was likely given that responsibility by the deceased person. If possible, family members in close proximity to the deceased should be involved in some decisions. Immediate children, spouses, siblings, and parents who are still living likely have a right to give their two cents on matters, but the person who was named executor of the estate has the final say.

Others may have different opinions on which items should be kept, which should be sold (and how or where to sell them), and which items should be donated (and to what charity). Some people may simply want to throw it all away, rather than spend the time to parse the possessions out into different categories. The most important advice I can give you when negotiating these decisions with other family members is to put the PEOPLE before the STUFF.

People over stuff.

Always.

No matter what happens with the stuff, remember that the relationship with those still alive is what is most important now. Your memories of your loved one who has died are not going to evaporate if you get rid of the stuff. Your memories of your loved one might be tarnished, however, if there is an all-out battle with other family members when clearing out the house. Don't let that happen. Take the high road, state your opinion, and if it comes to this, just let it go.

Sometimes, holding on to a loved one's stuff is the only thing keeping you together. Other times, letting go is the only way you can find peace. And you will have to find your own way of being at peace with this new reality you are living in, without your loved one. Everyone handles mourning and grief in a different way, so try not to be too judgmental or upset if others around you are handling it differently than you are.

Of course, a loved one's items do not replace the relationship that was lost, but they can provide comfort, a sense of connection, and reassurance during a difficult time. Keeping some of your loved one's items is very important but set limits for yourself – both a limit on how much stuff you will keep and a limit on how much time you will spend.

In the first weeks and even months, you may not be able to face sorting through the deceased's items. If or when months stretch into years, it's time to face the task of clearing out the estate. In the beginning, the tendency is to want to keep a lot of the stuff. That's okay. Keep as much as you have room for and be prepared to go through it again in a few years when you'll likely feel ready to let go of even more of it. Eventually, keeping just a box or two of items from those who have died will feel like enough. But not at first. That's okay. Give it time.

If you or a loved one are having a hard time thinking about how to disperse some of these items, sit down and make a list of who might be glad recipients. Friends, neighbors, co-workers, fellow congregants from your church, kids, grandkids, nieces, nephews, and other family members might make the list. You could even create a list of organizations that were near and dear to your loved one or to you. Creating a list like this will make you feel better as you tackle the task of donating the still-useful items left in the home of a loved one after they have died. Choosing worthy recipients will reassure you that these items will be put to good use. Knowing that art supplies, tools, or kitchen utensils can find a home, classroom or nonprofit where they will be used may inspire you to let go of even more stuff.

Throughout this process, people in your life will ask you how it's going. If your loved one resided in a small town or a close-knit community, others will be supremely interested in how the project is coming along. Be prepared to hear such things as "You're really going to get rid of all that?" or "How much stuff did you say you're keeping?" or "How long are you going to spend on this?"

In most cases, people aren't trying to be rude. They are curious, or they have been in the same position or they may be unsure of what to say to you about this difficult process. My advice would be to have an answer prepared so that you can put questions to rest quickly.

An example response might be, "It's been a difficult process, as you can imagine, but overall things are going as well as can be expected." This kind of phrase will help to end the conversation, as well as the idea that you are open to others' input on the sorting process.

Part II: Practical Tips for Letting Go

CHAPTER 4. BE PROACTIVE

We've spent the majority of the book this far talking about a situation in which a loved one has died, and the people left behind who must tackle the monumental task of emptying out the home and dealing with their loved one's possessions. However, you may be in a situation where you are trying to help your loved ones rightsize now, while they are alive. Or you may be looking at your own stuff and thinking that it's time to clean some of it out. Either way, the key to successfully letting go of the excess stuff is to be proactive. If you do the things outlined in this chapter now, you'll thank yourself later.

Rightsizing If Your Loved Ones Are Still Alive

If your parents, grandparents, or aunts/uncles are still alive, you have the opportunity to help them downsize proactively. Downsizing proactively can help them feel more comfortable (and even be safer) in their home so they can enjoy it more in their last years.

Ease the burden of clutter now

If clutter is accumulating in the main living areas (hallways, bedrooms, living room, bathrooms, kitchen), reducing the clutter can prevent trips, falls, bumps, bruises and even fires from happening. As people grow older, too much clutter around them not only weighs heavily on their minds, but, if it gets out of hand, can make the space around them downright dangerous. By helping your parents or others, you can make this burden so much lighter. Start by looking for items of little value in their home that they no longer need, use, or want: extra books, Tupperware containers, knick-knacks, clothing, towels, and anything else that is accumulating but has little emotional or monetary value. Donate, recycle or trash these items now to free up more space in your loved one's home.

Record the story of keepsake items

Some things will have high emotional or monetary value. While you are helping your loved ones downsize, you'll come across some of those high-emotion keepsake items that are important to your parents, important to you, or important to someone else in the family. Take the opportunity NOW to talk about the item, share the memories and stories associated with it. Consider writing a note to put on the back or bottom of the item (i.e. photo of Diane's great-grandparents when they got married; china tea set from Great Aunt Molly, who was born in 1870). If you do that, these items will be precious keepsakes after your loved ones are gone – not burdensome clutter. If the items have antique value outside of your family, knowing the provenance is also helpful if you ever choose to sell them.

If your loved ones are still alive, now is the best time to get them to tell you those stories and share those memories while they are still able to. Help them to see this sorting process as a positive one. Give them the gift of your time and attention. Keep the energy upbeat, take time to interact, appreciate the importance of the items, and listen to their stories. You may hear stories you've never heard before about objects that have surrounded you for decades.

For even more bonus points, record a video of your loved ones talking about the important keepsake items in their home. After they are gone, this video will be more of a treasured keepsake than the items themselves. It may be hard to believe now, but years or decades after your parents are gone, you will give anything to see their faces and hear their voices again. We all have a video camera at the palms of our hands these days, so put your smartphone to good use and start recording some memories.

Rightsizing Your Own Things Now

This clearing out process will also likely get you started thinking about your own belongings and how you can be proactive on sorting now so that you don't leave a burden of stuff behind for others to sort through. I call this process "rightsizing," the perfect place between too much and too little. When you are ready to get your possessions in order, keep in mind some of the following suggestions.

Set limits for yourself

This especially applies to keepsake items that are stored away in a box in your basement. My recommendation is always to use or display your keepsakes when possible, but some items invariably end up living in a box: keepsakes from your childhood, your high school days, your wedding, your own children's childhood, travels you have taken, cards and letters you have received. These are the keepsakes of life that start with good intentions but just continue to pile up year after year. After a few decades in a home, you look in your basement or attic and come to realize that you've accumulated 20 or more boxes of memory clutter.

So set a limit. You can cull down your collection of memorabilia from your childhood to one box. Your wedding? One box. Travels you have taken? One box. Things from your own children? One box per child. Go through those keepsakes regularly to try and really stick to those limits. What will happen is that by limiting yourself to a certain number of boxes for each category of "keepsakes," you will end up keeping the absolute best of the best (and ONLY the best).

What tends to happen if we keep EVERYTHING is that the best memories get diluted and the treasures we keep are much less significant (even burdensome). Force these limits on yourself and you'll keep only that which is truly meaningful.

Sort through your keepsakes often

Don't think that once you have sorted through your keepsakes one time that you are done. What you will find is that what was meaningful to you five or ten years ago may hold little significance to you now. Just because you've kept it for five, 10 or 15 years doesn't mean you have to keep it forever.

One example of this might be high school yearbooks. I have a yearbook from each year, 7th grade through 12th grade, plus four years of undergraduate college. That's 10 yearbooks! When I first got the yearbooks, they were supremely important to me, full of photos of people I knew and loved dearly. After 20 years, however, those memories tend to fade, and their significance get diluted by all the new memories I've made in the time since. For now, I will keep those yearbooks, but I can tell you this – when I downsize and move to a retirement community decades from now, you can bet they're not coming with me. And will my children want them? Of course not.

Break up sets

Another tip to remember is that it is okay to break up sets of things. Just because you want to keep a few items of a grouping doesn't mean you need to keep them all. Let's stick with the yearbook example – another good alternative would be to keep one or two yearbooks from your collection and get rid of the other eight, or if you have a set of china you inherited from your mother, it's okay to keep just a few place settings and let the rest of go. If you have a set of antique Victorian furniture passed down from a great-grandparent that really doesn't fit in your current home, it's okay to keep the chest of drawers and sell or give away the bed and dresser.

The same goes for collections. The problem with collections of any sort is that they are often more fun to accumulate than to have. The appeal of a collection is often in the thrill of the hunt, the seeking out and tracking down of various pieces for the collection. Once the items are collected, it's much less fun to see them sitting in a box or on a shelf. So, give yourself some grace and let go of a collection that is no longer giving you joy. Feel free to give away a collection that you inherited that gave someone else joy. Keep just your favorite piece – or five or ten pieces from the collection – whatever is reasonable for you to display and continue to enjoy having.

Articulate, in writing, who gets what and why

If there are items you own that you would like to pass on to your relatives or friends someday, consider making a list of who gets what, why that item is meaningful, and why you'd like them to have it. Share this list with your family members. There shouldn't be any surprises after you pass away. Remember that this is part of the legacy you are leaving behind you, so do this with care. Plan a family meal and invite everyone over. Have copies of the list for everyone and take the time to explain your choices.

If you are no longer using these items yourself, consider giving them to your loved ones NOW, before you die. Have someone take a photo of you with each of your loved ones and the items you are giving to them. That photo will be so much more treasured than any object could be, but having the photo of you, them and the object will make it much more likely that they will keep the item long term.

Finally, remember that just because you want to give a person an item doesn't mean they HAVE to take it. Be gracious if they do not. Remember that it doesn't mean they don't love or care about you.

Remember that this is not a competition

There are no awards to collect or accolades to be earned for having the greatest amount of stuff. You cannot win at being the most sentimental. Your loved ones will not value you more for having an unmanageable amount of stuff. Someone someday will have to deal with all of your possessions after you pass away. Don't let your belongings be a burden to them.

Rightsizing If Your Loved One Has Passed Away

If your parent/spouse/loved one has died and you are left facing what is left of their worldly possessions, please hear me loud and clear: This is now YOUR decision to make, not theirs. Or, if there are other heirs in the situation, it is a decision that must be made collectively and peacefully, if at all possible. Your loved one is gone and now you must step into the role of being a decision maker. Sometimes this is an easy transition to make, other times it is not. Perhaps you are not used to making decisions in the absence of your loved one, but now is the time to do so.

Ultimately, the thing to remember is this: Objects don't hold memories, people do. Keeping more objects won't bring your loved one back or make your memories any more vivid. The degree to which you loved the person who passed away is not reflected in how many of their items you keep. So, keep only what you will use, display and love. Let the rest go.

To help determine what you will keep, consider the following:

Of all their items, what makes you the happiest?

Which objects would make you smile each time you looked at them or used them? The wedding photo of your loved one, hanging in their hallway? The funny bobble head that sat on the kitchen windowsill? Your parents' record collection and record player?

What memories about this person stand out the most to you, and what objects are associated with those memories?

Did you cook or bake with your loved one? Could some of their kitchen items serve as a great memento of those memories you have? Perhaps the recipe box? Or maybe you went fishing a lot with your loved one – and you treasure those times? If so, for you, the fishing poles and a tackle box would be a good keepsake.

What items do you think are beautiful enough to display and have in your own home?

Have you always admired a painting that belonged to your loved one? Would you love to have it hanging in your living room? What about a gorgeous set of dishes that you would love to display in your china hutch and use for family dinners? What do *you* like? These may not be the items that have the highest monetary value but they may mean the most to you.

Try to only take items you intend to DISPLAY or USE. If you think something is lovely, but it will end up in storage because you have no place for it, don't take it.

Are there functional pieces you could actually use in your home?

Could you use another lamp in your guest room? Take one from your loved one's home. What about a crock pot? Or perhaps your loved one's snowblower is much newer and more powerful than the one you have. You might as well make use of some of the practical items that belonged to your loved one if they would fill a real need for you or someone in your family.

Hire a professional to help with the rest

After identifying which items you will keep and what you'll give to family members and friends, you'll then need to determine what will be done with what remains.

Do the items remaining in the home have high monetary value, or is most of it fairly worthless? Both scenarios are tricky in their own way. If the items in the home do have value, you may want to sell the items you don't wish to keep. You can do this yourself (selling online or having a garage sale) or you can hire a professional (auctioneer or estate sale company) who specializes in liquidating estates.

Think about how much your time is worth, and be careful how much time you spend on selling these things. You can easily end up spending several months trying to sell a few thousand (or even a few hundred) dollars' worth of items. If, however, you have pieces that have a significant value (several thousand dollars' worth), you will want to do your due diligence and ensure that you get a fair price for these items.

As someone who has run estate sales for the last 12 years, I can attest to the fact that some of us may have a few valuable items in our homes that could bring several hundred or several thousand dollars, but the majority of the STUFF in our homes is just that – STUFF. Even worse, it's *used* stuff! We live in a world that is filled with mass-produced goods, and the Internet has made it amazingly easy for buyers to access any kind of item they wish to buy, even antiques. That Depression glass your mother was so proud of? It can be found in most antique stores across the country, and hundreds of pieces can be purchased right now on eBay. The way any kind of value is determined in the marketplace is based on supply and demand, and the supply of such items has become so accessible via the Internet that demand is no longer a driving force.

So, think about the kinds of items you are letting go of, and ask yourself how rare are they *really*? Did most people of your parents' generation have them? Singer sewing machines, pump organs, fur coats and wooden toolboxes were very commonplace for people of a certain generation. Just because it's old doesn't mean it's valuable or rare. Remember that things were being mass produced as far back as the early 1900s.

The Internet has made it easier for collectors to buy, but it has also increased competition by making it more difficult for sellers to sell. If you're still having a difficult time coming to terms with what your keepsakes are worth, search for that item on various sites like eBay, Etsy, Craigslist and even your local Facebook Marketplace. You are likely to find several others selling the very item that you have.

In my work as a senior move manager, I have found that often it's the homes where there is little of monetary value that are the most difficult for family members to empty. If there is little monetary value in the contents of the home, the task will be to decide which items are worthy of donation and which items can be recycled. Then, the rest will be hauled to the trash.

You might need to hire some manpower to box up and haul these items to charities, recycle and trash facilities. In cases like these, you will spend more money to get rid of the stuff than you will make selling any of it. However, there are financial benefits to getting the job done in a timely manner. Remember that emptying out the home of your loved one will enable to you to sell the property, or to stop paying rent.

The cleanliness of the home is also a determining factor. Is the home dirty, dusty, musty, or inhabited by mice? Are the things in the home old, outdated, vintage, or antique? Things that are "old" or "outdated" likely have little value. Things that are "vintage" or "antique" might have some value.

Emptying out a home is an enormous amount of work, far more difficult than most people realize. For that reason, I want to encourage you to consider hiring professionals to help you make the process easier. Professional organizers, senior move managers, auctioneers, estate liquidators, appraisers, and junk haulers all make their living helping people who are emptying out a lifetime of accumulated stuff and can help you evaluate the potential value of the items in the home.

The resources are out there. Use them. Consider the cost in the same category as other services you need after someone passes away – funeral services, cemetery plots, obituary articles in the newspaper, realtor fees for selling the home, etc. Clearing out the residence is part of the process of tying up all the loose ends after someone leaves this earth. Help is out there, and it is money well spent.

CHAPTER 5. LETTING GO WITHOUT THE GUILT

Many of you may be reading this book because you already feel too burdened with the excess stuff of a loved one. You know you need to let go, but it's hard. You feel like you *should* keep an item (instead of donating it), you *should* want to display this item in your home (but it doesn't fit your aesthetic), or you *should* favor this item over something you already have in your home (but you don't). Perhaps you feel like you *should* be grateful to have all these precious items left over from your loved one (but it really feels like a burden).

You may feel that somehow all these items translate into memories and love and connection to the person who is now gone, so you can't let any of it go. But when it's too much – when you can no longer walk through your basement, when your garage is overflowing with boxes filled with someone else's memories, it's time to learn to let go and set some limits. It's time to resist having an emotional reaction and instead make a rational decision.

Let me be clear. You won't remember your loved one any better if you keep 50 boxes of their items or five boxes. The memories are inside of YOU, not inside of those boxes. Let me illustrate. Think of someone in your life who you've lost five or more years ago. Maybe it's a parent or a grandparent. Think about the items you have that belonged to that person. Now ask yourself, if you had 10 more boxes in your home, filled with stuff from their life, would it change the relationship you had with them? Would you be able to remember them more? Would you love them more? Would it mean that they had loved you more? Of course, the answer is no.

Stuff

$$\neq$$

Love

$$\neq$$

Memories

I keep coming back to this idea: your relationship with that person is what it was. As difficult as that can be to accept, you won't change anything by keeping more or less of their items. In fact, the number of items you keep from a loved one will have almost no bearing on your memories. I've worked with people who had a fabulous relationship with their departed loved one and chose to keep almost none of their stuff. I've worked with others who had a very troubled relationship with their family member and had a difficult time letting any of their stuff go.

When it comes to deciding what to keep, you've got to set a limit for yourself. Begin with the big stuff – furniture, cars, boats, and houses. Do you have a desire to keep any of these things, and is it reasonable to do so? Do you have enough space, time, and money to keep them? Next, move on to smaller items. When you are sorting, it is supremely helpful if you set a limit for how much you are willing to keep. Do you have room for five boxes of items? 20 boxes of items? More? Less?

I would challenge any client I was working with who stated that they wanted to keep MORE than 20 boxes of keepsake items for themselves. I would encourage them to edit more ruthlessly to condense the "keep" items to only the very best. After more than 10 years of experience helping family members sort through houses, I have found that a limit of three to five boxes of items is reasonable in most situations, but you get to choose. So be intentional and thoughtful about setting a limit for yourself, and then STICK TO IT.

The best items to keep will be items that you can either USE or DISPLAY in some way. The whole point of a keepsake is to remind you of a loved one and to bring you joy, right? So why not find a way to interact with these treasured objects on a daily or weekly basis? By keeping items you can USE (like a dining room table, a rolling pin, or a piece of jewelry), you can touch, see, and integrate those objects into your everyday life. You will (hopefully) get a warm and fuzzy feeling each time you use them.

Items that you keep on display have a similar effect. These items that can be hung on a wall, put into a shadow box, or kept in your home in a place of honor will make you smile each and every time you see them. Therefore, items that can be USED or DISPLAYED should always get top priority.

Items that you want to keep but will be stored away in a box should be kept to a minimum. I have these kinds of objects of my own – confirmation certificates, large family portraits (that I'm unwilling to hang on my wall, but still want to keep), birth certificates, newspaper clippings, letters, cards, and photographs. These items are still important to me, but do not have a place of honor in my home. They are kept in a sealed plastic tub in my basement, but there are only two of them (not 20). Remember, set firm limits for yourself, and stick to them.

Something else I've found in my work with clients and my own personal experience is that our attachment to objects changes over time. For instance, you may choose to keep your high school yearbook, the letters from your high school sweetheart, your graduation gown, the program from the graduation ceremony, or the embossed napkin from the reception. These items all seem very important when you are 18 and preparing to leave behind high school and strike out on your own for the first time. By the time you are 45 or 65, however, perhaps you would be content to keep only one or two of these items to remind you of your high school days. The rest can likely be tossed.

The same happens with our children, doesn't it? Especially for our first child, we may be tempted to keep every sweater, every piece of artwork, and every worksheet throughout their childhood. By the time that child has grown, however, we see the error of our ways and know that it's time to toss the math worksheets and finger paintings. Maybe we keep a baby blanket, a teddy bear, and a few pieces of artwork they made. That should suffice.

In this same way, I have found that our attachment to items that belonged to a deceased loved one releases its grip on us over time. In the beginning, we want to keep it all. As time goes on, we come to peace with a world in which our loved ones are no longer a part, and we create new memories and lives without them. It is at this point that we are able to set a limit and tell ourselves that keeping three boxes of items is enough.

It's hard, even after you've decided on a limit, to stick to it. I recommend developing some mantras, or encouraging phrases, that you can repeat to yourself throughout this process. I encourage you to come up with your own, but some suggestions might be:

"You can't keep it all."

"I don't want to live in a museum."

"These are wonderful memories, and I intend to continue creating even more memories by living in the present."

One of my favorites is "You can't move on to the next chapter if you continue re-reading the last one."

These mantras can also be helpful when responding to others when they question your process of sorting and getting rid of items.

If there are items you know you won't be keeping, either because they are only "kind of" special, or because you simply don't have room for them, take a photo of them. If that photo can be taken on location in your loved one's home, so much the better. The photo will continue to be treasured, and will trigger a memory for you without having to keep the actual item.

So, what can you do when you're sorting through a room and you're just not sure if you should keep something or not? Try to identify the emotions you feel when you see the object. Do you feel joy when you look at the item? Do you feel sadness? Guilt? Nostalgia? Regret?

I once worked with a client who was downsizing and moving out of the home she had shared with her husband, who had died. We were sorting through the items in his office and she came to his books and materials from Alcoholics Anonymous (he had been a recovering alcoholic).

"Oh, what should I do with these?" she wondered out loud.

I asked her if seeing them made her happy or sad.

"Well, they definitely don't make me happy," she identified.

"Then that's your answer" I said, gently. There's no sense in keeping an item that brings up painful memories.

I had to take my own advice when it came to a piece of glassware I had in my home. It had been part of my mother's collection, or it was meant to be. I had bought the glassware to give her for Christmas one year, but she died December 16, before I could give it to her. That glassware sat on a shelf in my home, along with the rest of the collection, for several years before I realized that seeing that one piece just brought up painful memories of my first Christmas without her. I kept the rest of her collection, which is on display in my home, but let go of that one piece.

If you are still having a hard time sticking to your limit, I'd encourage you to think about which objects serve as the best reminder of your loved one. Keeping fancy china is all well and good, but if the china was rarely used and was not a central part of your memories you had with this person, then I'd recommend passing on it in favor of items that spark more positive memories for you.

What's more valuable – a gold watch or a die-cast model tractor? If your father had a gold watch that he rarely wore, except to special events and occasionally to church on Sundays, it's okay to let it go. If your father loved farming and being out on the land and had a collection of model tractors, then for you keeping a few of his model tractors might be more representative of him and his life than his gold watch. It's okay to sell the watch and keep the tractor.

Consider the amount of space you have in your home for extra items. In every estate, there are usually some large items that can be difficult to know what to do with – pool tables, organs, looms, spinning wheels and more. In these instances, it's important to have a clear idea of how much of your own space you want to dedicate to keeping these items. However, merely having the space for an item is not reason enough to keep it. Remember that if you decide to keep something, you or your loved ones will eventually need to decide what to do with it after you are gone. Avoid delaying decisions until the next generation.

There are things that you feel like you can't throw away – military uniforms, Bibles and other religious paraphernalia, personal items like birth certificates, report cards, marriage certificates, and old photos. When emptying out a loved one's home after they die, my advice is to put these memorabilia items in a box and bring them to your home if possible or put them into storage. These are items that should be thoughtfully distributed and offered to members of your family, not items whose fate should be determined in the harried aftermath of a death.

Is it possible to box up these personal items in a reasonable number of boxes? 10 boxes? 20 boxes? If you can, then do it, and decide later. If there is an overwhelming number of items in this category and there is simply too much to box and store, then triage the pile of stuff and keep what you can store – whether it's five boxes or 20 boxes. You can come back to them at a later date, with a clear mind. Let the rest go, and don't beat yourself up about it.

Just because your loved one kept a huge amount of paraphernalia from the past doesn't mean you have to. Consider if there are local museums that would value these items. For yourself, set a limit and keep only the items you feel most strongly about. That is enough. It has to be.

What you are really doing when deciding which items to keep and which items to let go of is setting priorities. You are determining which belongings are more important to you than others. They can't all be important – because when everything is precious, nothing is. When you keep boxes and boxes of a loved one's items, the memories get diluted. A garage full of keepsakes from your deceased father isn't nearly as meaningful as two boxes of carefully selected items would be.

Another way we can limit ourselves is by thinking that keepsakes must be fancy or valuable to justify keeping. Not true. Sometimes the most casual, everyday items can be the ones most filled with memories of our loved ones. I have an old cardigan sweater hanging in my closet that belonged to my mom. It is not anything beautiful or fancy, and in fact was the sweater she wore only around the house and on the farm. My mother never would have gone "to town" in this sweater, but it's something she wore nearly every day of my childhood. It smelled like her for months following her death. To me, it is precious.

I like having it in my closet, but it won't mean anything to anyone else after I am gone.

So often we think of our fancy items as being worthy of passing down: our crystal goblets, our china dishes, our pricey figurines, and antique furniture. But it just may be the cookie jar, the cowboy boots, or the hammer from the garage that means the most to our remaining family members. Ultimately, when you are sorting through items and making decisions to "keep" or "discard," my advice is that if it's not a "HECK YES!" then it's a "NO."

When sorting gets you down and overwhelmed, it can be hard to keep going (or even to get started). So, my suggestion is to conquer the project 30 to 90 minutes at a time. Depending on your level of motivation, set a timer for 30, 60 or 90 minutes and tell yourself that you will work on sorting until the buzzer rings. Then, you can take a break or quit for the day. Or you may choose to keep going. Chances are that some days you'll be more than ready to quit and other days you'll keep going for two or three hours and make some real progress.

How do you eat an elephant? One bite at a time.

CHAPTER 6. IF YOU'RE GOING TO KEEP IT, KEEP IT WELL

Now that you've sorted and determined what items you want to keep, be intentional about keeping those items well. Remember, it's hard to love it if it's in a box. Take a careful look at all the keepsakes you've decided were important enough to bring home to your space. Now let's make sure they don't just sit in boxes in your basement, attic, or garage. Let's do something with them!

The primary goal should be to try really hard to USE or DISPLAY the majority of items you are choosing to keep. The reason you have kept these items is that they bring back good memories, so let's integrate them into your everyday life so that they can be a daily reminder of your loved one, or of happy times.

Here are some ideas on how to display special objects:

- Place small items into a shadow box that can be hung on a wall. These are available at craft stores, or you can have a custom shadow box made at a local frame shop.

- Add favorite old photos or flat papers such as newspaper articles or wedding programs to a photo album that can be easily stored on a shelf.
- Display a hand-written recipe in a frame in your kitchen.
- Make a quilt (or pay someone to make it for you) out of your loved one's clothing.
- Take old jewelry to a local jeweler and ask them to re-work the pieces into something more modern that you can wear and appreciate often.

Search for ideas online on how to display whatever kind of keepsake you have. Sites like Pinterest and Etsy are great for ideas. If you want to dig deeper into creative ways to save your items, I recommend reading *Past and Present: Keeping Memories of Loved Ones Alive* by Allison Gilbert. The book is filled with creative ideas that will help you find new ways to keep mementos.

Displaying or using family keepsake items have the additional benefit of exposing them to visitors or to other members of your family, including the next generation. If an object is out in the open, it's easier to talk about the item or to tell stories about where it came from and why it's important to you. Enjoy the opportunity to talk about the person who owned or made the item – and the significance it has to you. In this way, we allow our memories to be alive, not stale. We may even be able to create new memories around this item and our loved one who has passed.

Something that is important to remember is that if our children or grandchildren choose to keep an item in the family, they will only do so because of the way the piece relates to them personally. They won't hold onto something because you had pleasant memories of it – only if they do.

I have some items that belonged to my great-grandmother, my mother's maternal grandmother. She is a woman who died in 1965, long before I was born. She had a collection of "purple dishes" that she bought at auction for a few dollars, or so the story goes, and now they are supposedly worth a lot of money (however, my decade of experience in the estate liquidation business tells me that their actual monetary value is nominal at best).

My grandmother kept and displayed the dishes in her home after my great-grandmother died. My mother did the same thing after my grandmother died. When my mother died, it was easy to decide to keep those purple dishes that had been passed down through three generations of women in my family. However, let me be clear: I am not keeping those dishes because they remind me of my great-grandmother. She died decades before I was born, and I can't be reminded of someone I never even met. I kept the dishes because I remember them being important to my grandmother and my mother, and I am reminded of them when I see these dishes.

If my children decide to keep those purple dishes after I am gone, it will not be because of their memories of the first three generations of women who owned them (my mother, my grandmother and my great-grandmother). My children never met any of those women. They will keep those dishes only because they have memories of me keeping them, using them, displaying them, and talking about their significance.

So, if you wish to pass down items to future generations, talk about the items on a regular basis. By telling stories of the item or using the item, you are creating new memories for the next generation.

One of the most abundant areas of keepsakes will likely be photos, slides, and home movies. These can be overwhelming in many cases! My advice is to put all these kinds of items together in boxes and plan to go through them AFTER the rest of the estate has been sorted and liquidated. Photos, slides, and home movies take time to sort through, and the process shouldn't be rushed.

Once you are ready to tackle this project, the first step is to sort through the photos and discard those that you don't wish to keep. Yes, you read that right. You DON'T need to keep each and every photo your loved one took throughout their lives.

Some photos, slides and home movies are worth keeping, and some are not. For instance, scenery shots are fun to take in the moment but rarely last the test of time. If your loved one travelled to the Rocky Mountains in 1963, you don't need to keep every photo (or any photo) of a rock, tree, or wildlife that you find. Now, if there is a photo of your relative standing in front of the Rocky Mountains in 1963, with their 1960s clothing and hairstyle, and their 1960 Oldsmobile sedan, then that's the vacation photo to keep. Toss out the pine trees and the black bears and keep the people. Cull out the dull photos that don't spur an emotion for you so you can enjoy the photos that really do mean something.

As for slides and home movies, you may need to do a little work to find the proper equipment to be able to view these items. Once again, you may find that several of the slides your loved one saved are not something you need to keep. Do a Google search for "Convert slides to digital" with your city and state and you'll find many local services (and some national ones) that will convert your slides to a digital format. Some even allow you to view the slides after they are converted and delete any you don't want, without having to pay for them. Again, with slides, choose images of people rather than scenery or wildlife.

The same process goes for converting home movies to digital. Whatever format you have (8mm, VHS, or reel-to-reel), do a quick Google search for your area to find someone that can help you view or convert these home movies to digital so they can be kept for future use. You can also choose to sort home movies by titles or years. What is more valuable to you "Macy's Parade, 1960" or "Family Canoe Trip, 1974"?

The message of this chapter is to be thoughtful, intentional, and maybe even a little brutal in how you keep your keepsake items. If you're going to keep it, make sure you are keeping it well and in a way that you can find the item and enjoy it when you want to.

I recently worked with a client whose story illustrates why it's so important to keep something well if you're going to keep it at all. She had boxes and boxes (and boxes and boxes!) of items she had kept from her parents' house when it was emptied out. So many boxes, in fact, that there were entire rooms of her home that she couldn't use because they were full of her parents' things. She told me about a silly greeting card that her father and she had sent back and forth to each other for birthday celebrations for several years in a row. They would cross out the name of the last person who signed it and re-sign their name, then send it time and time again. It was a special memory she had of a man she dearly loved. I had hoped she had the card framed and hanging on a wall somewhere, but when I asked about it, she confided that she couldn't find it. It was somewhere in those rooms of boxes.

In her desire to keep it all, my client was really losing the few things that mattered the most to her. When you keep everything, nothing is really special. What is rare is precious, even when it comes to our keepsakes.

PART III: CREATING YOUR LEGACY

Chapter 7. Time Marches On

When it is your job to help people empty out their homes, or the homes of their loved ones, the circle of life is not an abstract idea. It is in your face, each and every day. As a senior move manager and estate liquidator, I am confronted with aging and mortality on a daily basis. My team and I see first-hand that no one lives forever, and that you can't take any of your STUFF with you when you go. Time marches on, and no one is getting out of this world alive.

I consider it a privilege to be faced with this lesson over and over again. Because I entered this field of work when I was a mere 28 years old, I have had the unique opportunity and blessing to view this transition from a generation or two removed from my senior clients. Many of the folks I helped in the past had grandchildren my age, and now that I am approaching the age of 40, many of my current clients have children that are my age. Someday I will be helping clients who are not that much older than I am. Time marches on.

I had the great privilege of being surrounded by older generations throughout my entire childhood. My grandparents were all born between 1910 and

1918, and all died between 1992 and 1994. We lived half a mile from one set of grandparents and one and half miles from the other. They were like second and third set of parents to me, and together my extended family formed a safety net woven with love and support and wisdom hard-won from experience. Our holidays included not only my immediate family and all four grandparents, but great aunts and uncles and other old folks who didn't have anywhere to go on holidays. My brother and I were often the only children, and we soaked it all in.

When all four of my grandparents died within two years, I watched my grandparents' houses be emptied out. After my mother's death in 2005 and my father's move off the farm and into town, I helped empty out my parents' house as well. In both my personal life and my career as a senior move manager, I have been able to experience and observe the grief process both up close and from far away. The one thing I've learned is that time marches on.

My husband and I were recently filling out a family tree for our children (ages 10 and 7) so they can see who their relatives are a few generations back. The first few branches of that family tree were easy to fill out – parent's names, grandparent's names. But then, it got a lot more difficult.

Can you name all four of your grandparents? You probably can. Going back one more generation, can you name all eight of your great-grandparents? Most people cannot.

I know more than many do about my own family history because it's something I am genuinely interested in. But even I could not name all eight great-grandparents off the top of my head. I had to look up the names in the records I have. Once I found them, I thought – "Oh yes, I remember hearing about that person."

My father is a huge history buff and was very interested in both his family tree and my mother's. He talked about the people, showed us photos, and connected a lot of dots.

My husband, on the other hand, did not have that experience growing up. He knew all four of his grandparents, but beyond that he wasn't able to name a single great-grandparent without first checking with his mother. And even then, books and records had to be consulted before we could really come up with even a few names. After much research, we were able to definitively identify only five of his eight great-grandparents.

All of this got me thinking about my own descendants and how one day even I will be forgotten. If this exercise taught me anything, it's that that day is coming sooner than I'd like to admit. My great-grandparents were born between 1859 and1894. The last one died in 1965. Only about 55 years have passed since my last great-grandparent died, *and I barely remember their names.* Now that is a sobering thought.

Am I an anomaly? Am I just an ungrateful kid who can't take the time to learn about her family's history, heritage, and roots? No, I don't think so. I think I'm pretty typical. In fact, I think I have more connection to my ancestors than a lot of people. I think we remain fairly connected to our great-grandparents while our parents are still alive, because of course our parents are more likely to remember their own grandparents and can share stories about them with us. But after our parents are gone, it becomes a lot easier to forget the generation that is three branches removed from us on the family tree.

This is an interesting perspective on life and the passage of time, especially when we think about our possessions and our hopes of passing on the "stuff" that is so very important to us. I don't think it means our stuff has no meaning. No, your stuff can and should matter to you, and some of it will matter to your children or grandchildren after you are gone. But your great-grandchildren? That's a bigger leap to make and the chances are greater that the meaning of your things will be lost. Time marches on.

New generations are born, and children grow up. Great-grandparents die, grandparents die, and parents die. Someday we too will die. It's the circle of life. When we lose a loved one, it seems as though our grief will never end. And maybe it doesn't, but it does change. Our attachment to STUFF doesn't help us to heal any faster. The keepsakes that we are attached to now likely won't mean much to the next generation and will mean even less to the next. But to the following generation? Our great-grandchildren? They may not even know our names. And they likely won't want much, or any, of our STUFF. And that's okay. Remember when you tried to name all eight of your great-grandparents? You probably couldn't do so either.

Time marches on. We need to accept that keepsakes may not last the test of time. They can mean something to us in the here and now, be important to us for a season or a chapter or a lifetime, and then fade away. This brutal truth and reality check can help us to hold on to our keepsakes with an open hand rather than a tight fist.

Chapter 8. What You Really Leave Behind

Your legacy is what you leave behind for your family after you die – and it's a whole lot more than stuff. You leave behind lessons, habits, beliefs, attitudes, recipes, even jokes and stories. Some of what you leave behind is good. Some of it may not be so good. But the totality of what you leave behind is your true legacy. Once you understand that, you can stop focusing so much on the STUFF and really spend time thinking about the true impact you are having in the here and now.

When I work with older adults who are downsizing, what they are really doing is editing their possessions down to what is most essential, most representative of their lives and what they hope to pass down. Consciously or not, they are really wondering: Did any of this really matter? What was it all for? My life, this place, my experiences, the things we did here – will anything be remembered? Will my lessons last? These are the questions that all of us ask when closing one chapter and beginning a new one.

Yes, our lives and experiences did matter – and do matter. For now. But time is fleeting, and our memories won't matter forever. Know that that's okay. Your legacy will be so much more than your stuff. It will be the values and patterns of behavior that you instilled in those around you that will have ripple effects. We distract ourselves by focusing on our stuff so that we don't think about the very real generational impact our lives have: inherited trauma or grief, positive or negative relational patterns, resilience and bravery, fear and cynicism, perseverance in all circumstances, helpfulness to strangers, stubbornness, or an attitude of thankfulness. *What are you passing on?* Your legacy is a whole lot more than just dishes, furniture, and a few collections.

We pass on health habits, spending habits, relationship patterns, worldviews, values, religious points of view – the list goes on and on. In my family, when I think of my great-grandparents, the biggest thing they did to impact my life was to immigrate to the United States from Norway. Had they not made that enormous change in their geography and culture, our family's life would be vastly different today. These kinds of legacies have a much larger impact on your family two, three or four generations down the line than your collection of stamps, Toby Jugs, or Hummel figurines.

Our attachment to stuff is a distraction, a crutch, often an excuse to ignore our true legacy. If you spend years of your life holding on to the past, what will that, in turn, pass down to those you leave behind? You could spend so much time treasuring another person's legacy that you neglect to build your own.

Leaving a positive legacy that endures can be done without a lot of stuff. In fact, I would argue that the best keepsakes aren't things at all. They are the games you remember playing with your grandparents as a child, the songs your uncle used to sing on Sunday mornings, the stories Dad told around the dinner table, the sayings your grandparents used, the recipes your mom made, the skills your father taught you. These are all examples of clutter-free legacies that have a lasting impact. They may even hang around years after your name has been forgotten.

So, be intentional about what you want to leave behind: faith, wealth, wisdom, values, stories, love, service – or STUFF? Choose wisely.

Our

legacy

is so much more
than our stuff.

Chapter 9. Sorry, Your Kids Don't Want Your Stuff

"My kids don't want my stuff!"

This is the bemoaning cry of an entire generation – the Baby Boomers. They dutifully kept the items their parents passed on to them when they died, and they can't believe their children of the Gen X, Gen Y and Millennial generations don't want this stuff.

Let me assure you that your children's love for you is not at all tied to how much of your STUFF they want to keep. Remember that love and memories are not the same thing as stuff.

Let me assure you that your children, grandchildren and loved ones will want some of your stuff. It just might not be what you expected, and it won't be much. In our society, the pendulum has swung towards a minimalist aesthetic, and consumers no longer view possessions as something they intend to keep for a lifetime.

If you really want your kids or grandkids to appreciate your stuff after you are gone, you must attach a story and/or an experience to it. If there is a single piece of pottery that came over from the "old country" with an ancestor, make sure it is prominently displayed in your home and talked about often. Use it, let family members see it and touch it and hold it. Let them know how and why it is important to you. If you do that, chances are much higher that it will be kept in the family for another generation or two.

Often the items that family members end up keeping are everyday items that are attached to experiences shared – woodworking tools or rolling pins, or a classic car you used cruise in together. What is really being kept here is the experience, which created a memory in your loved ones' mind. The object itself is merely representative of that experience.

To most effectively leave behind keepsake items, you must have a reason for why you want future generations to cherish these items. The hand tools that belonged to your grandfather may represent hard work. The handmade quilt made from scraps by your great-grandmother may represent sacrifice or thriftiness. The set of china that was brought out for every family meal may represent the importance of family gatherings. Talk about these items and tell the story about them. When items are attached to an important family value or a memorable experience, they become meaningful. Don't expect your children to love a ceramic bear collection just because you found the bears cute.

When you are thinking about passing down items from your ancestors, remember to create your own memories with family members as well. Don't just re-live others' memories; create memories for your children, grandchildren, nieces/nephews, neighbors, and friends. Focus on the connections and relationships that are in your life NOW, not just the ones that are gone.

Perhaps those generations that have gone before you have done a great job leaving a meaningful legacy that goes beyond just STUFF. Or maybe they have not. If that is the case, be proactive about your own legacy with your family members and friends. Learn from your experience and do better.

It is my intention to leave the legacy of appreciating keepsakes but not living in the past. I hope that my children and grandchildren keep a healthy balance of appreciating memories and keepsakes from my generation, while not placing too much of an emphasis on my possessions. I want my legacy to be so much more than my stuff.

Give the kids
your story
not your stuff.

CONCLUSION

I had a moment of clarity the other night while playing a card game with my 10-year-old daughter. She and I often play a hand or two of cards before bed, and this night we were playing a game my grandfather taught me called "Golf."

My grandfather passed away in 1994, at the age of 82. I was 12 years old at the time. I have fond memories of playing cards with my grandfather. Those memories have been reinforced by stories I've heard from other family members. Every time we brought out the cards, my parents or other relatives would mention my grandfather and say, *"He could remember every card the players at the table laid down!"*

I started to look around my house to see what objects I have that belonged to my grandfather, and I wasn't able to come up with much. I have an old milk can from his farm, which I use as a piece of decor in my basement living room. I have plenty of photos of him and his family, but that's about it. I have more keepsake items from my grandmother, but not as much from my grandfather specifically.

But here's what I realized, the other night, playing cards with my daughter. This card game that my grandfather taught me 30 years ago is the best memento I could possibly have of him. I think of him each and every time I play it, and I can't help but get a little choked up when I reflect on what he would think of me playing it with my own daughter in the year 2021.

My grandfather, Clyde Larson, is my children's great-grandfather. He was born in 1912 and died in 1994. My children were born in 2011 and 2014. Forty years from now, when my children are in middle age, they will scratch their heads and try hard to come up with the names of all eight of their great-grandparents, and they will likely fail. Just the thought of this brings tears to my eyes. However, when I take a step back and try to recall all eight of my great-grandparents, I can't. I have no emotional connection to them. They died decades before I was born, and all I have is a few scattered stories I've heard, along with a few precious objects. That's enough.

What's more important that I do have is the knowledge of how those eight people, all of whom lived 100+ years ago, impacted my life. I would not be here if it were not for them. They are the ones who came to the United States from the old country. They are the ones who joined a new church, moved to a new state, and set up a homestead on the farmland that still sustains my extended family. It's the intangible things that they left behind that matter, not their dishes, quilts, or knick-knacks.

The best memories don't always come from objects. A keepsake doesn't have to be a thing. It can be an activity, a feeling, or a lesson. It could be music you listened to together, or old movies you watched with one another. For me, episodes of "The Golden Girls" and the movie "The Sound of Music" are keepsakes. They remind me of my mother, who watched these with me multiple times during my adolescence. When I share these very same shows with my daughter, it makes me warm inside, knowing that she will look back on these times and remember me when she is grown and I am long gone.

I hope that the advice in this book has given you permission to make choices to let stuff from the past go. Let go of the things that are weighing you down, the items that don't make you happy, the stuff that is distracting you from the here and now. Keep some of it, but only the best.

Remember that scarcity makes something precious. If you keep just one box of items from your deceased

PERMISSION SLIP

I, _____ give myself
permission to let go of _____
___China_____
___Keepsakes that don't make me happy__
___Old collections_____
___Anything that's not a "Heck Yes!"__
signed _____

loved one, the items in that box will be precious. If
you fill up your basement or garage or storage unit
with boxes and boxes of things from your loved one,
the stuff will be a burden – the very opposite of
precious.

Time is scarce. They're not making any more if it.
We are only here for a short number of years. Make
the most of them and don't waste your time, space, or
energy on keeping excess stuff. Your loved one's
belongings won't bring you happiness, contentment,
or peace. Focus your time and attention on the here
and now, on your experiences, and on your current
relationships. The quality of your relationships now

define how you will be remembered and valued.
Your family and friends will not love you because of
the stuff you leave behind. They will love you
because of the memories you made.

ABOUT THE AUTHOR

JEANNINE BRYANT is an expert at helping older adults and their loved ones through times of transition. As the owner of a senior move management company in Lincoln, Nebraska, she has helped hundreds of older adults through the rightsizing process, taking them by the hand and walking them from start to finish through the transition to a smaller residence. Jeannine has a passion for helping others understand the benefits of rightsizing their homes and belongings. She lives in Lincoln with her husband and two children.

Visit www.EasyRightsizing.com for more rightsizing tips and information.

Visit www.ChangingSpacesSRS.com to learn more about Changing Spaces SRS, Jeannine's senior move management company.

VISIT WWW.EASYRIGHTSIZING.COM FOR FREE COMPANION RESOURCES

*Clutter-Free Gift Ideas
*The Power of Counting Worksheet
*What to Keep When a Loved One Dies
*Tips to Make Your Loved One Feel at Home in Their New Space

…And many more videos, blog posts and tips offered about the rightsizing journey!

ONE LAST THING...

If you enjoyed this book or found it useful, I would be very grateful if you'd post a short review on Amazon. Your support really does make a difference. I read all the reviews personally so that I can receive your feedback and make future books even better.

Thanks again for your support!

Made in the USA
Coppell, TX
17 February 2022

73700429R00053